'Laughter is timeless, imagination has no age and dreams are forever' - Walt Disney

A child's imagination knows no boundaries. Children have an innate ability to imagine and create stories from scratch and are always looking for new ideas and experiences to understand the world around them.

These "Would You Rather? – Totally Gross Edition" questions will stimulate your kids' imagination and bring out some amazingly hilarious, rather gross and interesting answers.

This book is a great tool to :

*• **Improve communication** by encouraging your children to talk and express themselves freely while discussing their choices in a fun and light-hearted way.*

*• **Encourage critical thinking** : these questions will help children develop hypotheses about the different scenarios and encourage them to think in new and different ways.*

*• **Stimulate imagination and creative thinking** through our list of ridiculous and totally gross scenarios.*

*• **Strengthen relationships** by spurring healthy and interactive discussion in a fun and care-free environment.*

*• **Nurture curiosity and improve general knowledge** with our list of unique and quite "random" facts.*

*P.S : These questions are "**Kid-Friendly**" and are an excellent idea to get the conversation started!*

Welcome !

Thank you for purchasing my book!

My name is Alfie, I'm an indie author and a full time parent.
I've been working on creating fun and educational games, stories and books for kids for the past couple of years.

As a parent of two, finding ways to entertain the kids while teaching them how to think, communicate and learn important values has been one of my top priorities.
Developing curiosity and creative imagination has become crucial to adapt and grow in today's society.

I really hope you enjoy this book, and if you do, please consider leaving us a review sharing your experience, 'd love to read it and I'd really appreciate it!

MEET ROTTER !

He's a sweet and cuddly zombie! He gets usually shy around new people, but once he gets to know you, he will become your best companion!

Rotter lives a lot of wacky and crazy adventures, and has an offbeat sense of humor, never failing to offer a good gag or to provoke laughter. Rotter enjoys the simple things in life, like brain cakes, zombie toys and other gross things.
But most importantly, he loves making his friends laugh with his silly, ridiculous jokes and rather gross puns. He likes to cuddle and spend time with the people he cares about the most.

How to Play ?

- *Play with minimum two players* : *Choose at least one other player besides yourself to play the game. If you have a large group of people, you can play around in a circle or even form teams.*

- *Choose the first player who will ask a question that begins with "Would you rather...?" and provide the two scenarios for the second player to choose from.*

- *The second player has to choose <u>only one scenario</u> – and explain why ?*

- *If one of the players says "eww" or express their disgust when playing the game, they get a penalty point. At the end of each round, the player with less penalty points wins the round !*

- *<u>REMEMBER !</u> the questions and scenarios featured in this book are solely for entertainment purposes, and should not be taken seriously !*

Most importantly, have fun, laugh and enjoy your time with your family and loved ones!

Round 1

WOULD YOU RATHER ?
(make sure to explain why?)

eat a chilli flavoured beetle
or...
a vinegar flavoured worm?

EWW POINT __ /1

EWW POINT __ /1

want to burp every five minutes
or...
sneeze every ten minutes?

WOULD YOU RATHER ?

(make sure to explain why?)

eat a mouldy sandwich you found on the floor
or...
lick the bottom of a dustbin?

EWW POINT ___ /1

EWW POINT ___ /1

eat an earth worm that still has soil on it
or...
a cockroach that just climbed over a rotting apple?

WOULD YOU RATHER ?
(make sure to explain why?)

always sneeze out boogers or...
have a string of snot hanging out of your nose for a month?

EWW POINT ___ /1

EWW POINT ___ /1

let everyone in a room know that you are about to fart or...
let everyone know that you are going to the bathroom to do a number two?

WOULD YOU RATHER ?
(make sure to explain why?)

lay on a floor that had mouldy food on it
or...
lick a countertop that had a rat crawl over it?

EWW POINT ___ /1

EWW POINT ___ /1

have to sleep next to a smelly skunk all night
or...
spend a day sitting at a garbage dump?

WOULD YOU RATHER ?

(make sure to explain why?)

drink water from a glass that still had soap at the bottom of it

or...

from a glass that had slime down the side of it?

EWW POINT ___ /1

EWW POINT ___ /1

eat mud

or...

lick the bottom of your shoes at the end of a day?

Score Board

Player 1 Name   **Player 2 Name**

---------- VS ----------

Penalty Score

---------   ---------

THE WINNER !

Round 2

WOULD YOU RATHER ?
(make sure to explain why?)

*have to smell your whole family's socks every evening or...
your best friend's armpits every evening?*

EWW POINT ___ /1

EWW POINT ___ /1

*not wear deodorant for a full week or...
not brush your teeth for a full week?*

WOULD YOU RATHER ?
(make sure to explain why?)

PLAYER 1

not wash your hair for two weeks
or...
not wash your body for two weeks?

EWW POINT ___ /1

EWW POINT ___ /1

PLAYER 2

wash your body with snail slime
or...
with mud?

WOULD YOU RATHER ?
(make sure to explain why?)

eat strawberry flavoured boogers
or...
eat strawberries that have boogers on them?

EWW POINT ___ /1

EWW POINT ___ /1

have bubble-gum stuck in your hair
or...
stuck between the pages of your schoolbooks?

WOULD YOU RATHER ?

(make sure to explain why?)

pee your pants every afternoon when you are at school

or...

poop your pants every morning when you wake up?

PLAYER 1

EWW POINT ___ /1

EWW POINT ___ /1

PLAYER 2

lick your own sweat from your armpits

or...

eat your own boogers?

WOULD YOU RATHER ?
(make sure to explain why?)

chew on a slimy worm for five minutes
or...
quickly chew and swallow a dung beetle?

EWW POINT ___ /1

EWW POINT ___ /1

eat an over ripe banana that is black
or...
drink sour milk?

Score Board

Player 1
Name

Player 2
Name

_____ VS _____

Penalty Score

_____ _____

THE WINNER !

Round 3

WOULD YOU RATHER ?

(make sure to explain why?)

> *lick a toilet seat*
> *or...*
> *lick a toilet brush?*

EWW POINT ___ /1

EWW POINT ___ /1

> *not wipe your bum for an*
> *entire week*
> *or...*
> *not bath for a full week?*

WOULD YOU RATHER ?
(make sure to explain why?)

not change your underwear for a week or...
not change your socks for two weeks?

EWW POINT __ /1

EWW POINT __ /1

have hair covering your whole body or...
scales covering your face?

WOULD YOU RATHER ?

(make sure to explain why?)

take a bath only once a month
or...
sweat whenever you go outside?

EWW POINT __ /1

EWW POINT __ /1

hold a slimy eel
or...
a wet octopus?

WOULD YOU RATHER ?
(make sure to explain why?)

hold a handkerchief that someone else blew their nose into

or...

hold a baby's dirty diaper?

EWW POINT ___ /1

EWW POINT ___ /1

have a stranger puke on your feet

or...

walk barefoot through a dirty public bathroom?

WOULD YOU RATHER ?
(make sure to explain why?)

shake someone's hand that did not wash their hands after using the bathroom
or...
shake someone's hand who just wiggled their finger in their nose?

EWW POINT __ /1

EWW POINT __ /1

put your finger in someone else's nose
or...
cut their toenails for them?

Score Board

Player 1
Name

Player 2
Name

VS

--------------- ---------------

Penalty Score

------------ ------------

THE WINNER !

Round 4

WOULD YOU RATHER ?
(make sure to explain why?)

lick someone else's toes or... wash their dirty underwear?

PLAYER 1

EWW POINT __ /1

EWW POINT __ /1

sit in a bath of rotting vegetables for two hours or... sit in a garbage dump for a day?

PLAYER 2

WOULD YOU RATHER ?
(make sure to explain why?)

have a baby pee in your face whilst changing their nappy
or...
have them throw up all over your new pants?

EWW POINT __ /1

EWW POINT __ /1

lick the floor of a busy shop
or...
the wall of a prison cell?

WOULD YOU RATHER ?
(make sure to explain why?)

eat a worm on its own
or...
drink a slippery slug that is
mixed with juice?

EWW POINT __ /1

EWW POINT __ /1

drink sour milk
or...
a glass of concentrated
lemon juice?

WOULD YOU RATHER ?
(make sure to explain why?)

wash your body with rotten brussels sprout soap
or...
with a bar of soap that is full of worm juice?

EWW POINT __ /1

EWW POINT __ /1

lick the slimy trail of a snail
or...
eat a mouldy, soft tomato?

WOULD YOU RATHER ?

(make sure to explain why?)

be trapped in a puddle of boogers from a troll

or...

in a puddle of ear wax from a giant?

EWW POINT ___ /1

EWW POINT ___ /1

have someone sneeze in your hair

or...

sneeze in your face?

Score Board

Player 1
Name

Player 2
Name

VS

-------------   ------------

Penalty Score

--------   --------

THE WINNER !

Round 5

WOULD YOU RATHER ?
(make sure to explain why?)

PLAYER 1

*burp for a whole week
or...
fart for a whole week?*

EWW POINT ___ /1

EWW POINT ___ /1

PLAYER 2

*help someone burst their
pimple
or...
help them clean their
nose?*

WOULD YOU RATHER ?
(make sure to explain why?)

*lick a dog's bum
or...
lick a cat's bum?*

EWW POINT ___ /1

EWW POINT ___ /1

*poop in the cat's litter
box
or...
poop in the neighbour's
garden?*

WOULD YOU RATHER ?

(make sure to explain why?)

be friends with a flesh-eating zombie

or...

be the enemy of a flesh-eating zombie?

EWW POINT __ /1

EWW POINT __ /1

eat a cockroach that is still alive

or...

eat two dead cockroaches?

WOULD YOU RATHER ?
(make sure to explain why?)

slip and fall into someone's pee or... slip and fall into dog poop?

EWW POINT ___ /1

EWW POINT ___ /1

wash a dead body or... sit next to a dead body for an entire day?

WOULD YOU RATHER ?

(make sure to explain why?)

> *eat spaghetti that is made from earth worms*
> *or...*
> *eat spaghetti that is made from stringy boogers?*

EWW POINT ___ /1

EWW POINT ___ /1

> *lick someone's shoe that stepped in dog poop*
> *or...*
> *lick someone's shoe that stepped in horse poop?*

Score Board

Player 1 Name   **Player 2 Name**

---------- VS ----------

Penalty Score

____   ____

THE WINNER !

Round 6

WOULD YOU RATHER ?
(make sure to explain why?)

lick a dirty carpet that has not been cleaned in a year
or...
sleep in a bed full of crawling bed bugs?

EWW POINT __ /1

EWW POINT __ /1

touch your own eyeball
or...
touch someone else's eyeball?

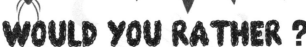

WOULD YOU RATHER ?
(make sure to explain why?)

eat soup that has eyeballs in it
or...
eat soup that has zombie fingers inside it?

EWW POINT ___ /1

EWW POINT ___ /1

drink a vampire's blood
or...
drink the juice of fifty beetles?

WOULD YOU RATHER ?

(make sure to explain why?)

*eat a dead mouse
or...
eat a dead scorpion?*

EWW POINT ___ /1

EWW POINT ___ /1

*have fifty cockroaches
climb over your face
or...
have twenty large spiders
climb over your feet?*

WOULD YOU RATHER ?
(make sure to explain why?)

sleep in a room that has
mud dripping from the
walls
or...
in a room that has slime
on the floor?

EWW POINT ___ /1

EWW POINT ___ /1

eat a grasshopper
or...
a raw prawn?

WOULD YOU RATHER ?

(make sure to explain why?)

eat a slithering baby snake
or...
a crawling scorpion?

EWW POINT ___ /1

EWW POINT ___ /1

chew on a piece of
rotting wood
or...
chew on someone else's
bubble-gum?

Score Board

Player 1 Name

Player 2 Name

--------------- VS ---------------

Penalty Score

------------   ------------

THE WINNER !

Round 7

WOULD YOU RATHER ?
(make sure to explain why?)

*lick the tyre on a car
or...
lick the tyre on a truck?*

EWW POINT ___ /1

EWW POINT ___ /1

*swallow worms whole
or...
poop them out whole?*

WOULD YOU RATHER ?

(make sure to explain why?)

lick a stranger's hands
or...
a stranger's feet?

EWW POINT __ /1

EWW POINT __ /1

sleep in a sleeping bag
full of maggots
or...
sleep in a tent full of
spiders?

WOULD YOU RATHER ?

(make sure to explain why?)

PLAYER 1

lick a frog's head
or...
lick a skunk's bum?

EWW POINT ___ /1

EWW POINT ___ /1

PLAYER 2

drink sea water
or...
drink water from a muddy river?

WOULD YOU RATHER ?

(make sure to explain why?)

brush your teeth with a
toothbrush made of
cricket's legs
or...
a toothbrush made of
bird's claws?

EWW POINT __ /1

EWW POINT __ /1

wash your body with a
sponge covered in dirty
hair
or...
with a sponge covered in
mould?

WOULD YOU RATHER ?
(make sure to explain why?)

take a bath and only wear dirty underwear
or...
not be able to take a bath but get to wear clean underwear?

EWW POINT ___ /1

EWW POINT ___ /1

sit in a bath that has sour milk in it
or...
take a shower that has sour milk come out of it?

Score Board

Player 1
Name

Player 2
Name

---------- VS ----------

Penalty Score

....

THE WINNER !

Round 8

WOULD YOU RATHER ?
(make sure to explain why?)

PLAYER 1

> eat a poisonous snake
> or...
> pet a poisonous frog?

EWW POINT ___ /1

EWW POINT ___ /1

PLAYER 2

> drink an entire glass of
> your own sweat
> or...
> eat something a baby has
> chewed and spat out?

WOULD YOU RATHER ?
(make sure to explain why?)

PLAYER 1

find a dead rat in your refrigerator
or...
find a dead rat in your bed?

EWW POINT ___ /1

EWW POINT ___ /1

PLAYER 2

eat a rotten potato
or...
a raw potato?

WOULD YOU RATHER ?
(make sure to explain why?)

eat food that has dirt on it every day
or...
drink water that has dirt in it every day?

EWW POINT ___ /1

EWW POINT ___ /1

eat food that your sibling spat into
or...
drink water that your sibling spat into?

WOULD YOU RATHER ?

(make sure to explain why?)

have an itchy armpit
or...
have an itchy bum?

EWW POINT __ /1

EWW POINT __ /1

lick used coals
or...
lick burnt firewood?

WOULD YOU RATHER ?
(make sure to explain why?)

use a very dirty toilet that cannot flush
or...
poop in your pants?

EWW POINT __ /1

EWW POINT __ /1

have a huge pimple on your nose
or...
a huge pimple in the middle of your forehead?

Score Board

Player 1
Name

Player 2
Name

---------- Vs ----------

Penalty Score

_____   _____

THE WINNER !

Round 9

WOULD YOU RATHER ?

(make sure to explain why?)

> *sweat heavily under your armpits*
> *or...*
> *always have a runny nose?*

EWW POINT ___ /1

EWW POINT ___ /1

> *lick your own armpit that has been sweating all day long*
> *or...*
> *lick between your toes that have been in smelly socks all day?*

WOULD YOU RATHER ?
(make sure to explain why?)

lick your friend's scabs or...
lick inside your friend's ears?

EWW POINT __ /1

EWW POINT __ /1

pee your wants every time you laughed or...
laugh uncontrollably every time you peed?

WOULD YOU RATHER ?
(make sure to explain why?)

fart the entire time you are at a sleep over with your friends
or...
need to use the toilet regularly to poop?

EWW POINT __ /1

EWW POINT __ /1

drool while you are sleeping
or...
fart while you are sleeping?

WOULD YOU RATHER ?
(make sure to explain why?)

take a bath in water that smells like sewage or... take a bath in dirty water?

EWW POINT __ /1

EWW POINT __ /1

lick your own ear wax or... lick your own bum?

WOULD YOU RATHER ?

(make sure to explain why?)

lick inside an elephant's ears
or...
be farted on by a dinosaur?

EWW POINT ___ /1

EWW POINT ___ /1

eat a chocolate that tastes like boogers
or...
eat boogers that smell like chocolate?

Score Board

Player 1
Name

Player 2
Name

----------- VS -----------

Penalty Score

_____   _____

THE WINNER !

Round 10

WOULD YOU RATHER ?
(make sure to explain why?)

smell your grandmother's bum
or...
smell a baby's poop nappy?

EWW POINT ___ /1

EWW POINT ___ /1

finger paint a picture with colourful snail slime
or...
with a mashed, rotten carrot?

WOULD YOU RATHER ?

(make sure to explain why?)

have dandruff fall from your hair into your food

or...

fall into your juice?

EWW POINT ___ /1

EWW POINT ___ /1

cook with sour milk

or...

cook with old oil?

WOULD YOU RATHER ?
(make sure to explain why?)

> *drink a glass of vinegar*
> *or...*
> *a glass of olive oil?*

EWW POINT __ /1

EWW POINT __ /1

> *eat rotten tomatoes in*
> *your salad*
> *or...*
> *eat sea slugs in your*
> *salad?*

WOULD YOU RATHER ?
(make sure to explain why?)

> *always have bad breath*
> *or...*
> *have bad body odour?*

EWW POINT ___ /1

EWW POINT ___ /1

> *have fleas crawling down*
> *your pants*
> *or...*
> *have lice in your hair?*

WOULD YOU RATHER ?
(make sure to explain why?)

eat two cups of dry dog food
or...
one cup of wet cat food?

EWW POINT ___ /1

EWW POINT ___ /1

have your entire body covered in long hair
or...
be completely bald from head to toe?

Score Board

Player 1
Name

Player 2
Name

---------- Vs ----------

Penalty Score

___ ___

THE WINNER !

Round 11

WOULD YOU RATHER ?
(make sure to explain why?)

have toes instead of fingers
or...
fingers instead of toes?

EWW POINT __ /1

EWW POINT __ /1

kiss an octopus
or...
kiss a jelly fish?

WOULD YOU RATHER ?
(make sure to explain why?)

get caught scratching your privates
or...
caught digging in your nose?

EWW POINT __ /1

EWW POINT __ /1

sneeze out yoghurt every time you sneezed
or...
fart out chocolate syrup every time your farted?

WOULD YOU RATHER ?
(make sure to explain why?)

have burps that smell like farts
or...
farts that are as loud as burps?

EWW POINT ___ /1

EWW POINT ___ /1

have honey pour out of the shower
or...
mayonnaise pour out of the shower?

WOULD YOU RATHER ?
(make sure to explain why?)

never be able to take a bath again
or...
never be able to brush your hair again?

EWW POINT __ /1

EWW POINT __ /1

eat three live cockroaches
or...
have fifty cockroaches living in your bed?

WOULD YOU RATHER ?

(make sure to explain why?)

> *have a big piece of meat stuck in between your front teeth*
> *or...*
> *have a stringy booger hanging out of your nose?*

EWW POINT ___ /1

EWW POINT ___ /1

> *have an itchy rash on your bum*
> *or...*
> *an itchy rash underneath your armpits?*

Score Board

**Player 1
Name**

**Player 2
Name**

---------- VS ----------

Penalty Score

_____ _____

THE WINNER !

Round 12

WOULD YOU RATHER ?
(make sure to explain why?)

walk barefoot into dog poop
or...
walk barefoot through itchy, poison ivy plants?

EWW POINT ___ /1

EWW POINT ___ /1

drink a smoothie made from rotten fruit
or...
a drink a smoothie made from sour yoghurt?

WOULD YOU RATHER ?
(make sure to explain why?)

*smell like rotting meat
when you sweat
or...
smell like rotten eggs
when you run?*

EWW POINT ___ /1

EWW POINT ___ /1

*find cockroaches in your
box of cereal
or...
moths in your box of
cereal?*

WOULD YOU RATHER ?
(make sure to explain why?)

have a hundred flying locusts fly out of your fridge when you open it
or...
find your toilet full of scorpions when you need to use the bathroom?

EWW POINT __ /1

EWW POINT __ /1

eat an omelette made from rotten eggs
or...
drink a milkshake made from sour milk?

WOULD YOU RATHER ?

(make sure to explain why?)

PLAYER 1

find termites in the beach sand
or...
find fleas in the beach sand?

EWW POINT ___ /1

EWW POINT ___ /1

PLAYER 2

dream about becoming a booger
or...
dream about becoming a giant ball of ear wax?

WOULD YOU RATHER ?
(make sure to explain why?)

wake up to having peed in your bed
or...
wake up too late to make it to the bathroom and pee in the kitchen?

EWW POINT ___ /1

EWW POINT ___ /1

share your friend's sweaty gym towel after sports
or...
share your friend's smelly socks after sports?

Score Board

Player 1 Name   **Player 2 Name**

---------- VS ----------

Penalty Score

_____   _____

THE WINNER !

Round 13

WOULD YOU RATHER ?
(make sure to explain why?)

pee sour milkshake
or...
poop peas every time you
used the bathroom?

EWW POINT ___ /1

EWW POINT ___ /1

eat a rotten egg
or...
fart the smell of rotten
eggs for three days?

WOULD YOU RATHER ?
(make sure to explain why?)

have to wear shoes that walked through cat poop or...
socks that had dog pee on them to school every day?

EWW POINT ___ /1

EWW POINT ___ /1

fart clouds of dust or... sneeze out spaghetti?

WOULD YOU RATHER ?

(make sure to explain why?)

find a dead rat in your shoes
or...
a dead mouse on your pillow?

EWW POINT __ /1

EWW POINT __ /1

eat a fried spider
or...
a fried mouse?

WOULD YOU RATHER ?
(make sure to explain why?)

find fingernails in your pasta
or...
toenails in your soup?

EWW POINT __ /1

EWW POINT __ /1

have sticky boogers coming out of your ears
or...
have bad smelling ear wax dripping out of your nose?

WOULD YOU RATHER ?
(make sure to explain why?)

be trapped in a giant's saliva
or...
in a giant's ear wax?

EWW POINT __ /1

EWW POINT __ /1

stick your own smelly sock in your mouth
or...
lick the bottom of your shoes?

Score Board

**Player 1
Name**
**Player 2
Name**

VS
---------- ---------

Penalty Score

....

THE WINNER !

- - - - - - - - - - - - - - - - - - - -

Round 14

WOULD YOU RATHER ?

(make sure to explain why?)

PLAYER 1

bite your own dirty toenails
or...
bite your own dirty fingernails?

EWW POINT ___ /1

EWW POINT ___ /1

PLAYER 2

eat some else's boogers once a day
or...
never get to eat the food you enjoy ever again?

WOULD YOU RATHER ?
(make sure to explain why?)

eat ants that taste like
pepper sauce
or...
eat pepper sauce that is
made from ants?

EWW POINT ___ /1

EWW POINT ___ /1

always look great but smell
like rotten eggs
or...
smell like flowers and
always look bad?

WOULD YOU RATHER ?
(make sure to explain why?)

be chased by hundreds of angry bees
or...
get trapped in a cave with ten smelly skunks?

EWW POINT ___ /1

EWW POINT ___ /1

fart continuously for an hour after every meal
or...
burp uncontrollably for thirty minutes after every meal?

WOULD YOU RATHER ?

(make sure to explain why?)

eat a cake that had
worms inside of it
or...
eat worms that had cake
frosting on top of them?

EWW POINT ___ /1

EWW POINT ___ /1

have to use leaves to wipe
your bum
or...
use newspaper to wipe
your bum?

WOULD YOU RATHER ?

(make sure to explain why?)

> *find ants in your bath towel*
> *or...*
> *find fleas in your bath towel?*

EWW POINT ___ /1

EWW POINT ___ /1

> *be stuck in mud that had dog poop inside of it*
> *or...*
> *be stuck in sand that was full of termites?*

Score Board

Player 1 Name   **Player 2 Name**

VS

---------------   ---------------

Penalty Score

___   ___

THE WINNER !

Round 15

WOULD YOU RATHER ?
(make sure to explain why?)

have to eat the sourest food
or...
the spiciest food for every supper?

EWW POINT __ /1

EWW POINT __ /1

go to school with a bad haircut
or...
go to school wearing dirty clothes every day?

WOULD YOU RATHER ?
(make sure to explain why?)

smell like cat pee
or...
smell like dog poop?

EWW POINT ___ /1

EWW POINT ___ /1

stick your finger in a
giraffe's nose
or...
in an elephant's ear?

WOULD YOU RATHER ?
(make sure to explain why?)

*eat soggy biscuits
or...
eat slimy tomatoes?*

EWW POINT ___ /1

EWW POINT ___ /1

*eat toothpaste flavoured
sweets
or...
drink water that tastes like
toothpaste?*

WOULD YOU RATHER ?
(make sure to explain why?)

eat a cookie that has cockroaches in it
or...
a waffle that has wasps in it?

EWW POINT ___ /1

EWW POINT ___ /1

have someone sneeze all their spit onto the back of your neck
or...
have someone blow their nose on your shirt?

WOULD YOU RATHER ?
(make sure to explain why?)

lick a meat flavoured ice cream
or...
eat an ice cream that has octopus tentacles inside it?

EWW POINT ___ /1

EWW POINT ___ /1

have a dinosaur sneeze on your head
or...
an elephant fart next to you?

Score Board

Player 1 Name　　　　　**Player 2 Name**

---------- VS ----------

Penalty Score

....　　　........ ....

THE WINNER !

Congratulations !

You succeeded at this ridiculous & quite gross decision making challenge !

I hope you enjoyed playing this game. If you did, I would really appreciate if you leave us a review sharing your experience and stories. <u>It would mean a lot !!</u>

If you haven't done so already, make sure to check out my other books and follow my author's page on Amazon for future releases !

Till next time,
Witty Alfie

Witty Alfie
BONUS ACCESS

Join our fun club and get bonus monthly access to our giveaways & extras !

All you need to do is send us an email to *WAPublishingGroup@gmail.com* with the title "AMAZING ALFIE" – submit one ridiculous "Would You Rather..?" question and get :

- An entry to our monthly giveaway to win **up to 50$ Amazon Gift Card** !

- Access to our **free extras** !

A winner with the best submission will be picked each month and will be contacted via email.

Best of Luck !

Printed in Great Britain
by Amazon

59641104R00068